# A KILLING SNOW

# A KILLING SNOW

PAUL CILIFO

*A Killing Snow*
first published 2011 by
Scirocco Drama
An imprint of J. Gordon Shillingford Publishing Inc.


Scirocco Drama Editor: Glenda MacFarlane
Cover design by Terry Gallagher/Doowah Design Inc.
Author photo by Sandra Regier, Photographer
Printed and bound in Canada on 100% post-consumer recycled paper.

We acknowledge the financial support of the Manitoba Arts Council and The Canada Council for the Arts for our publishing program.


Production inquiries should be addressed to:
Paul Ciufo
Box 1198, Grand Bend, ON  N0M 1T0
www.paulciufo.com

Library and Archives Canada Cataloguing in Publication

Ciufo, Paul, 1970-
A killing snow/Paul Ciufo.

A play.
ISBN 978-1-897289-66-2

I. Title.

PS8605.I94K54 2011 C812′.6 C2011-904643-1

J. Gordon Shillingford Publishing
P.O. Box 86, RPO Corydon Avenue, Winnipeg, MB  Canada  R3M 3S3

## Acknowledgments and Dedication

Many creative and generous people helped me with the script. Eric Coates' enthusiasm and ideas were essential. Thanks to Kate Lynch, Shawn Kerwin and the rest of the remarkable cast and crew of the premiere production. Thanks also to those who took part in a workshop at Blyth Festival in snowy December 2009 including Tony Munch, Marion Day, and Barbara Fulton. Much gratitude to Duncan McGregor, Dr. Allen Middlebro', Jason Kayes, Louise Fagan, Michael Hew, Janet Anstead, Bill Carmichael, Judy & (the late great) Ed Cohn, Randall Lobb, Dave Scott, Rick Hundey, John Greig, Trish MacGregor, Jeff & Carli McLaren, and Gillian Fagan. Thanks to great friends and supporters Joan Karstens and Trish Trenter. Thanks very much to Gord Shillingford and Glenda MacFarlane for their interest in my work. Much love and thanks to Julie, Celia and Brynn.

*For my mother, Anne, who always figures out whodunit by page two but was stumped by this script (or so she told me).*

## Paul Ciufo

Paul's play *Reverend Jonah* was a finalist for the 2008 Governor General's Literary Award. *Reverend Jonah* premiered at the Blyth Festival and was published by Scirocco Drama. Paul's full-length radio drama *On Convoy* was produced and broadcast by CBC Radio. *On Convoy* was originally a stage play produced by Goderich Little Theatre Company. In July 2011 Paul's play *Narcisse* was produced by the St. Joseph and Area Historical Society. He is currently working on a film script entitled *Fortunate* and a memoir play called *The Sun Shines on Manhattan*. Paul lives in Grand Bend, Ontario, with his wife Julie and their daughters Celia and Brynn. For more information about Paul's writing, see www.paulciufo.com.

## Production History

*A Killing Snow* was commissioned by Eric Coates for the Blyth Festival. The play premiered on June 25, 2010, with the following cast:

| | |
|---|---|
| ALENA | Catherine Fitch |
| LIBBY | Patricia Hamilton |
| CALLIE | Lisa Norton |
| JACK | Gil Garratt |
| GERALD | Sam Malkin |

Directed by Kate Lynch
Set and Costume Design by Shawn Kerwin
Lighting Design by Rebecca Picherack
Sound Design by Todd Charlton
Stage Manager: Shauna Japp
Assistant Stage Manager: Crystal MacDonell

## Notes

The actresses can serve as the voices of the Fates. Music should be drawn from the Kronos Quartet's *Night Prayers*.

## Time and Place

December 27-31, 2007, a house in the country near the town of Clinton, Huron County, Ontario, Canada.

# Act I

## Scene 1 – Storm-Stayed

*The wind shrieks.*

*Faint afternoon daylight during a snowstorm illuminates a modest, open concept house.*

*In the kitchen is a wood stove, stack of wood, stove pipe disappearing up into the ceiling.*

*A large window through which can be seen only wind-driven snow.*

*A plain kitchen table with four chairs.*

*In the living room, a couch with a red blanket draped over it, an armchair, no TV.*

*Bookcases from floor to ceiling filled with books, mostly History and Latin texts.*

*Part of the living room serves as an office, with a desk, computer, a chair (with wheels), filing cabinet. A large whiteboard mounted on the wall is covered with notes scrawled in black marker; at the top in large letters is "**Fata**"; a tray for markers including a red one. The whiteboard is housed inside a wooden frame with hinged doors; it is on an angled wall and can be seen from the kitchen and living room. Tacked up on a bulletin board is artwork depicting the Fates. There is a globe on the desk.*

*Two doors: one exits offstage to a hall (leading to a*

*washroom and two bedrooms offstage.) and the other exits offstage to a mud room (There are two doors offstage in the mud room—one leads outside, the other to the garage).*

*Offstage in the mud room, the door to outside opens, wind howls louder for a moment, door slams shut, wind noise diminishes; a woman stamps her feet, gasps for air.*

*ALENA enters, agitated, freezing. She is sixty, haughty, carries a fashionable bag, wears fashionable clothes that are impractical given the weather.*

*She rushes to warm herself at the wood stove.*

*She grabs the phone and punches in 9-1-1. Waiting for the call to go through, her eyes fall on the books; she reacts with surprise and curiosity. She notices the whiteboard.*

ALENA: *(Astonished.)* Fata!? *(Into phone.)* Oh, yes, there's been an accident; a woman is dead... No... I'm not sure; on Airport Line, south of Clinton... What do you mean?... That's not acceptable! Perhaps you didn't hear me...? What exactly do you suggest we do? *(Hangs up.)* Useless!

*Offstage sounds of someone else entering the mud room from outside.*

*LIBBY enters. She is in her late fifties, plain, practical, salt-of-the-earth.*

*Beneath her heavy winter coat, she wears jeans and a hand-knitted sweater. She carries a purse and wears thick wool socks—having left her boots in the mud room.*

*(To LIBBY.)* Horrible.

LIBBY: *(Upset.)* She was a sweet lady.

ALENA: You knew her?!

LIBBY: Mrs. Sturgeon.

ALENA: I'm so sorry. I'm Alena.

LIBBY: Libby.

*Offstage someone else enters mud room from outside, slams door.*

CALLIE: *(Offstage.)* Brutal!

*CALLIE enters. She is twenty-eight, brainy, a chip on her shoulder. Dressed casually, wears her boots, totes a backpack.*

ALENA: It's bloody Siberia out there.

CALLIE: Worse, it's bloody Huron County.

LIBBY: The stove throws a good heat.

CALLIE: Did you call the cops?

ALENA: They're not coming.

CALLIE: What!?

ALENA: They've closed all the roads.

CALLIE: No! Shit! The guy made me come in, said I'd have to give a statement.

ALENA: He didn't seem thrilled at having to come to our rescue.

LIBBY: Crusty!

CALLIE: She was an older lady, apparently?

LIBBY: She'd be pushing eighty.

CALLIE: What was she doing out on a day like today?

LIBBY: I never seen whiteouts so bad.

ALENA: Atrocious. I'd think I was heading straight, and suddenly find myself about to plunge into the left ditch.

CALLIE: Whoa! We're in the house of a scholar.

ALENA: Indeed.

*Offstage a man bangs his way into the mud room from outside.*

Maybe this is him now.

*Offstage sounds of a man coughing, kicking off his boots. JACK enters. Mid-twenties, devil-may-care, almost always amused. Under his winter coat he wears navy blue winter overalls.*

JACK: All of youse make it in alright?

ALENA: Is the owner of the house coming?

JACK: Nah, he's busy making snow angels.

LIBBY: Jack?

JACK: Yeah? Libby?! What are the chances?

CALLIE: Seriously, where is the guy? I got to go.

JACK: We're coming up the laneway and he goes, "I got to head back".

CALLIE: We're sure the lady is dead?

JACK: Guy said she wasn't breathing and didn't have no pulse; guess that was his first clue.

ALENA: It couldn't have been the impact; we were just creeping along.

JACK: Took a heart attack from the stress, maybe?

*Sounds offstage of a man entering the mud room from outside.*

CALLIE: Finally.

*GERALD enters. He is sixty, wears a parka with a big hood that hides his face. He has left his boots in the mud room.*

ALENA: Hello—

GERALD: What were you thinking?! Do you place no value whatsoever on your own lives?! Idiots! *(Grabs the red blanket from the couch, stomps back over to the mud room door, exits.)*

JACK: Good meeting you, too.

*GERALD enters, without the red blanket.*

ALENA: So sorry to have pulled you out into that hellish weather.

LIBBY: That was real brave; a person could get lost out in that.

JACK: Or freeze his nuts off.

*Although GERALD's face is hidden by his hood, it is clear he is attempting to glare a hole right through JACK.*

CALLIE: Look, I got to go—

GERALD: —They've likely closed the roads.

ALENA: Yes, they have.

GERALD: *(Rips off his hat, scarf, parka.)* You're damned lucky. I just happened to look out the window and there was a lull, just for a second, so I spotted all of your four-ways flashing. Otherwise…

LIBBY: Gerry?!

GERALD: Libby? Of all the people…

JACK: Hey! Mister G.!? It's me Jack…Jack Van Bakel.

GERALD: Oh I know.

ALENA: Oh…my…God. *(Takes off her hat and scarf, revealing her face.)*

GERALD: Alena?! I was sure I knew that voice.

CALLIE: Same old Huron County everybody knows everybody and their dog.

ALENA: I don't live here; I have a cottage on the lake. Gerry and I went to university together, back when dinosaurs roamed the Earth.

GERALD: The eminent Dr. Petr, here in my humble home… wonders never cease. You look fabulous, as always.

ALENA: You've aged rather gracefully yourself.

CALLIE: This is fascinating, but what's the plan here?

GERALD: I didn't catch your name?

CALLIE: Callie.

GERALD: Callie, a woman is dead.

LIBBY: It's Mrs. Sturgeon, right?

GERALD: Yes, Iris Sturgeon.

LIBBY: She was my kindergarten teacher. She always told us, "You are not "kids"; "kids" are baby goats. You are people."

GERALD: I've heard she was a fine teacher.

*Frustrated, CALLIE goes to the desk, searches for a pen and paper.*

ALENA: We were all travelling separately but Mrs. Sturgeon and the three of us… *(Indicates herself, LIBBY, JACK.)*

JACK: Convoyed up.

ALENA: I suppose we owe you our thanks, for taking the lead.

JACK: I'm up higher, in the truck. I could make out the yellow line for a bit, then I had to go by the phone lines, then it just got stupid. *(Indicates CALLIE.)* Then I seen her, stopped. Don't know how I didn't plough right into her.

ALENA: So that's what happened!

CALLIE: I couldn't help it. There was a great, big gust—I was driving totally blind. Here's my cell number, for the cops. *(Heads toward mud room.)*

GERALD: It's getting worse, not better. The laneway has filled in. Even if you find your way back to your car…the police, not even snowmobilers can get around in this.

JACK: But snowmobilers would give 'er a go; we're crazy like that.

CALLIE: You don't understand I'm not spending a minute more than I have to in this godforsaken part of the world.

LIBBY: This part of the world is my home, thanks.

GERALD: Next time, check the forecast. It's a massive system; they're calling for this to last for days.

CALLIE: Days!?

JACK: Even if the snow lets up, there's tons of it on the fields. Until that wind dies down…

LIBBY: We're storm-stayed, but good.

*The reality of the situation sinks in. All are deflated.*

CALLIE: *(To LIBBY.)* Sorry about what I said, okay? It wasn't a whole lot of fun for me growing up around here.

GERALD: Whatever possessed all of you to get behind the wheel? Mrs. Sturgeon had a stack of Boxing Week flyers on the seat beside her.

JACK: Had to get out and get her deals! P-T-O shaft went on my snow-blower; kind of needing that working today. And I was hoping to pick up some Tink's Sixty-nine; it's on special.

ALENA: "Tink's Sixty-nine"?

GERALD: You really don't want to know.

JACK: Buck lure. You know, for hunting. Basically, it's deer piss. From a doe in rut. You put it on to mask your scent, draw in a buck. Works like a charm.

ALENA: You pay good money for…deer urine…and douse yourself with it?

CALLIE: So the buck is running toward you thinking you're a doe in rut…ever wonder what happens if your gun jams?

JACK: Never hunt alone.

ALENA: *(Quietly, to GERALD.)* You live among barbarians.

LIBBY: I was only out because my daughter really needed me.

JACK: What's wrong with Trisha? Her and Snappy split up?

ALENA: "Snappy"?

GERALD: He's a photographer.

LIBBY: *(To JACK.)* How did you know?

JACK: Clinton…all we got is a feed mill and a rumour mill.

ALENA: Tough time of year for a break-up.

LIBBY: He didn't want to do it before Christmas.

ALENA: So he waits until the twenty-seventh!?

LIBBY: Asshole.

GERALD: Libby!

LIBBY: He's not the first to break her heart.

JACK: There's two sides to every story.

LIBBY: You cheated; what's the other side of that?

JACK: You really want to get into this?

LIBBY: Trisha told me not to drive, but I wanted to give her a great, big hug.

ALENA: My kids couldn't make it home for Christmas. Again. With all the snow we've been getting, the cottage was beyond desolate. I just needed to be around some friends.

JACK: We'll be your friends.

ALENA: Oh goody.

CALLIE: I drove up from Toronto this morning, and was heading right back. Some family business to attend to…settling my aunt's estate.

*LIBBY suddenly looks quite ill and upset.*

JACK: Ah, you're from the Big Smoke. Explains a lot.

CALLIE: I grew up around here.

GERALD: *(To CALLIE, indicating JACK.)* Never wrestle with a pig. You get all dirty, and the pig likes it.

ALENA: *(Indicates whiteboard.)* Working on a paper?

GERALD: A book, actually.

ALENA: *(Picks up a notebook from his desk.)* A book! On the Fates, obviously.

GERALD: It's early days yet.

*GERALD takes the notebook from ALENA, puts it up on a high shelf. He firmly shuts the whiteboard doors.*

ALENA: You'll be retired now—lots of time to devote to it.

JACK: That big, fat teacher's pension. They say there's getting to be more retired teachers than there are senior citizens.

CALLIE: You're a veritable fountain of information.

ALENA: Was there ever a Mrs. Goldie?

GERALD: Never married. You?

ALENA: Three times married, three times divorced. Imagine how much more I could've published if I'd had your discipline.

GERALD: As if I have anything to teach you about discipline or publishing.

CALLIE: *(With distaste.)* You're not Mr. Goldie, the History teacher?

GERALD: History and Latin.

CALLIE: I've heard of you.

ALENA: *(Laughs.)* Nothing good, obviously. I've inherited a number of his students over the years, and they seem to have barely survived him.

GERALD: If you mean I made them work hard, prepared them…

ALENA: Oh, you prepared them alright; they found the university workload downright relaxing. I understand you made them take a quiz or a test every single class.

JACK: Yeah, we used to call him "Goldfinger", like the bad guy in James Bond. *(Sings.)* "Goldfinger..."

GERALD: *(Doing a slow burn.)* I see now I should've left you all to freeze in your cars.

JACK: I'll never forget the time Ferris Wheel—

ALENA: —Ferris Wheel? That's his name?!

JACK: His parents are a little different. So, first day, Grade Nine History, Ferris goes, "How many passed last year?" and Mr. G. goes "Everybody..." *(Pause.)* "except eight." Ferris gets all happy for a second, then whammo!

GERALD: That's just about enough.

JACK: Aw, come on Mr. G., don't get your shorts in a knot.

GERALD: You may call me Mister Goldie. Or since you're no longer a student Gerald. *(To CALLIE and ALENA.)* And you two—you're leaving puddles on my floor. I'll thank you to keep your boots in the mud room.

*CALLIE and ALENA slouch to the mud room door, pull off their boots.*

LIBBY: Can I use your phone? My family will be worried sick.

GERALD: Go ahead.

*LIBBY tries the phone, can't get a dial tone. She looks more and more distraught and ill. GERALD grabs a wad of paper towels to clean up the floor.*

CALLIE: *(Staring into mud room.)* What the...? Tell me that isn't...look, on the bench!

ALENA: Oh my God.

JACK: What? You got to be kidding me! You brought the body in?

GERALD: I covered her with a blanket.

JACK: That's weird, dude.

LIBBY: Sorry, I'm having trouble…

GERALD: Are you alright?

LIBBY: Not so hot. Can I use your washroom?

GERALD: Just down the hall.

*LIBBY takes a step and collapses; GERALD manages to catch her.*

Whoa!

JACK: Yikers!

GERALD: Libby? Libby?

ALENA: What's wrong with her?!

GERALD: How am I supposed to know? She feels all clammy.

JACK: When you're super-cold and come inside, your body can go all wonky.

GERALD: She wouldn't have gotten that cold walking from her car to here.

ALENA: *(Grabs phone.)* I'll call 911…not that they can send anybody! Damn, I can't get a dial tone.

GERALD: Phones must be out.

ALENA: I couldn't get any cell reception in the car.

*ALENA, CALLIE, JACK try their cell phones, to no avail.*

JACK: Nothing.

GERALD: There's no tower for miles, and it's very hilly around here.

CALLIE: Bloody Dark Ages.

JACK: How about sending an email?

GERALD: My service is through the phone line.

LIBBY: Oh… Oh…

GERALD: Libby!

ALENA: Thank God.

LIBBY: Oh, goodness…

GERALD: Get her some water.

*JACK fetches a glass of water.*

LIBBY: I'm all woozy.

GERALD: You're alright. Here, take a drink. Good. You gave us quite a scare.

LIBBY: Did the snow stop?

GERALD: Uh…you were only out for a minute; it's still snowing and blowing to beat the band.

LIBBY: *(Horrified.)* Oh no. Oh no!

GERALD: What's wrong?

*All are startled as GERALD's notebook flies off the shelf and bangs to the floor.*

CALLIE: Whoa!

ALENA: That didn't fall; it flew! *(Scoops up the book.)*

GERALD: Give me that.

ALENA: "One life-thread is cut; five more intertwine..."

GERALD: *(Grabs book from ALENA.)* That's private; it's my book research.

ALENA: I've never come across those lines before.

GERALD: Strangely, neither have I. And this isn't my handwriting...which is impossible.

ALENA: What's the rest of it?

GERALD: "One life-thread is cut: Five more intertwine; To form a knot that will bind and unbind."

LIBBY: The snow has to stop. We all got to leave. Right away!

*Blackout.*

## Scene 2 – Night Approaches

*The wind shrieks.*

*About fifteen minutes has passed.*

*CALLIE peruses the books, casts curious glances at the closed whiteboard.*

*ALENA reads a book, also glances at the closed whiteboard.*

*JACK tilts back on a kitchen chair, staring at the door to the mud room.*

CALLIE: "A room without books is as a body without a soul."

ALENA: Cicero. You should always source your quotations.

JACK: Speaking of bodies, we got to talk to Mr. G. about you-know-who. She's giving me the willies.

*They all look toward the mud room.*

Wonder if there's anything to eat in here. *(Rifles through kitchen cupboards.)*

ALENA: Make yourself at home.

CALLIE: Which book did you pick?

ALENA: *Metamorphoses*. I never tire of Ovid.

CALLIE: *The Twelve Caesars*. It's been too long since I picked it up.

ALENA: Good old Seutonius. You're a student?

CALLIE: Yeah. You're a prof?

ALENA: Classics.

CALLIE: I hope to say the same, someday.

JACK: "Veggie Chips"? You got to be kidding me. *(Tears open bag, eats.)*

CALLIE: I'm two courses, or a thesis, shy of my Master's. At my age you probably had your PhD.

ALENA: How old are you?

CALLIE: Twenty-eight. Just turned.

ALENA: At twenty-eight I had my PhD and I was already an Associate Prof.

JACK: Not too shabby.

ALENA: But everyone finds their own path.

JACK: *(Offers chips.)* Want some?

ALENA: I'll pass.

CALLIE: I have to work full-time; I don't get any help from my family.

ALENA: Same here, but I was fortunate with scholarships. Don't give up.

*CALLIE is clearly stung by ALENA's words.*

JACK: *(Mockingly.)* Words to live by.

ALENA: You're a farmer?

JACK: Proud of it. Plus I do a bit of modeling on the side.

ALENA: You're having me on. You're a farmer, slash, model? Are you in the Sears catalogue or something?

JACK: Been there, done that. But, you know that big ad for Passionfire Diamonds, with the guy in a lip-lock with a smokin' hot red-head?

CALLIE: That's you?

JACK: What can I say? God made me handsome.

ALENA: Unbelievable. *(Beat.)* Don't tell me you're a pig farmer?

JACK: Can't you tell from the smell? *(Indicates overalls.)* Guess these are new; got them for Christmas, along with a new pair of manure-proof boots.

ALENA: So you are a pig farmer.

JACK: That's "swine herdsperson".

ALENA: I don't know if I can stay in this room.

JACK: Too high-class for you?

ALENA: You pig farmers are destroying the thing nearest and dearest to my heart: my beloved Lake Huron.

JACK: Nah, that's not us; that'd be your septic tank. *(Sits in a kitchen chair.)*

CALLIE: I can't help myself. *(Goes to whiteboard, opens the doors a bit.)*

ALENA: *(Joins CALLIE.)* We really shouldn't.

JACK: "Make yourself at home".

GERALD: *(Enters from hallway.)* What do you think you're doing?

CALLIE: Uh…

GERALD: And you—get out of that chair.

JACK: Me?

GERALD: Nobody uses that chair.

JACK: Is this your "Special Seat"?

GERALD: No, I sit there. Best to avoid it, too.

JACK: So what's the deal with this one?

GERALD: If you have a problem with the house rules, there's the door.

JACK: Any special tiles we shouldn't be stepping on? A mug we shouldn't drink out of?

ALENA: How is Libby?

GERALD: She is resting.

ALENA: What got into her? She seemed downright panicked.

GERALD: No idea.

JACK: Maybe she was freaked out by…oh I don't know… her dead teacher hanging out in the mud room? *(Ghostly voice.)* "You are not baby goats; you are people."

ALENA: The body cannot stay.

GERALD: It can, and it shall.

JACK: Why not haul her right in here, prop her up by the stove?

GERALD: Have some respect!

ALENA: Maybe if we understood why you felt the need to…

GERALD: A hundred years ago people didn't run to funeral homes. A body was cleaned and displayed in the home.

ALENA: Gerry.

GERALD: *(Beat.)* If you must know, I couldn't bring myself to leave her out there. Alone. In the cold. I just couldn't. OK?

CALLIE: She is dead.

GERALD: I realise that!

JACK: Well, now we're euchred. We put her outside, nobody will find her 'til April.

LIBBY: *(Enters.)* We need to do something for her.

GERALD: Go lie down.

LIBBY: She deserves a service, a couple of prayers, something.

ALENA: Is that what upset you before, the situation with her?

LIBBY: No.

JACK: Don't know if this has anything to do with it but… she's a psychic.

CALLIE: Really? Did you see something?

GERALD: Don't tell me you believe in that nonsense?

CALLIE: Even the Caesars consulted sibyls.

JACK: "Sibyls?"

ALENA: Oracles.

JACK: "Oracles"?

GERALD: Prophetesses!

CALLIE: *(To LIBBY.)* What did you see?

JACK: Nothing happy, I'm thinking. And she's been right before.

CALLIE: Obviously something so bad, she thinks we should all leave. But we can't; the Fates oppose it.

*The lights go out leaving the room very dark, just a bit of light from the wood stove.*

LIBBY: Hey!

ALENA: What happened?!

GERALD: Everything's gone dead; the power is out.

LIBBY: This is bad!

GERALD: We're OK for heat, that's the main thing. I'll round up some light. Van Bakel, lend a hand? *(Clicks on a flashlight.)*

JACK: Where are we headed?

GERALD: The garage, off the mudroom. I'll protect you from Mrs. Sturgeon.

*JACK grabs the flashlight, holds at chin level and shines upward, gives a mock-evil laugh.*

*(Grabs back flashlight.)* Give me that.

ALENA: Such a child!

LIBBY: Could you leave a light for us?

GERALD: I've just got the one in here, but we won't be a minute.

*GERALD and JACK grab their coats, exit into mudroom.*

JACK: *(Offstage.)* Mrs. S.! How are you now?

GERALD: *(Offstage.)* Leave her in peace.

*Offstage sound of them going through door to garage.*

LIBBY: We've got to get away from here.

ALENA: Everything's going to be fine.

LIBBY: No. I got a bad feeling. Real bad.

CALLIE: We're in danger? From what, or who?

LIBBY: I can't say.

*Offstage sounds of GERALD and JACK entering mud room, taking off their boots.*

*GERALD enters, with three battery-powered camping lanterns. JACK enters, carrying an armload of firewood.*

GERALD: Success.

*Unnoticed by all, CALLIE exits down the hall. GERALD clicks on the three lanterns and they light the space brightly. JACK stacks the wood beside the stove.*

LIBBY: Thank goodness.

GERALD: Jack gets the credit. I thought I knew where I put them, but I was wrong.

JACK: Not bad for a...what did you call me the one time? "A dumb farmer".

LIBBY: That's terrible.

GERALD: I said no such thing.

JACK: You did so. Wanted to know why I was bothering to take Latin, told me I was your worst student ever.

GERALD: Worst behaved, maybe. I must've just been trying to motivate you.

JACK: Whatever lets you sleep at night. *(Beat.)* Heh, where is "Feisty"?

LIBBY: I didn't even notice…Callie? Callie!?

CALLIE: *(Enters.)* Heh.

LIBBY: Don't do that!

CALLIE: What? Nature called. *(Beat.)* If not him, who was your worst student?

GERALD: Tough to say; so many to choose from. *(Beat, to LIBBY.)* If you'd like to go out and say a few words for Mrs. Sturgeon, I'd be glad to go with you.

JACK: Me too.

CALLIE: Yeah.

GERALD: Then, unfortunately, we'll have to start thinking about dinner, and sleeping arrangements. *(Motions toward the hall.)* You women are welcome to the beds; Jack and I will bunk out here.

LIBBY: I don't care where you put me—I won't sleep a wink.

*Blackout.*

## Scene 3 – A Bloody Nightmare and Caesar's Words

*The wind shrieks. Total black.*

LIBBY: *(Screams.)* Ahhhhhhhh!! No! No!!

GERALD: What...?

LIBBY: Blood!

GERALD: What the...?

*GERALD jumps up, clicks on a lantern. He wears plaid, flannel pyjamas. He has been sleeping on the couch.*

*LIBBY stands near GERALD's desk, trembling.*

*Unnoticed by all, the whiteboard is open, all of the notes have been rubbed out, and printed in huge, red letters is IACTA ALEA EST. The red marker is missing.*

LIBBY: The blood!

GERALD: It's alright.

LIBBY: No, no.

GERALD: It's just a bad dream.

*ALENA and CALLIE enter from the hall.*

ALENA: What's going on!?

LIBBY: Everywhere. Blood. The walls. Pouring down.

CALLIE: What the hell?

GERALD: *(Helps LIBBY to a chair.)* Here, sit down.

CALLIE: Where's Jack?

GERALD: He was sleeping right there.

ALENA: Maybe he's in the washroom? *(Calls.)* Jack?

GERALD: Jack! *(Beat.)* Somebody go check.

CALLIE: You go.

GERALD: *(Indicates LIBBY.)* Stay with her. *(Steps toward hallway.)* Jack!

*JACK suddenly springs up from behind the woodstove, still inside a sleeping bag, wearing pyjamas like GERALD's.*

JACK: Huh?

*ALENA, CALLIE, and GERALD let out screams / startled yells.*

Ahhhh! What's everybody squawking about?

ALENA: You scared the hell out of us!

JACK: I scared you?

GERALD: What are you doing back there?

JACK: I got chilly.

ALENA: Didn't you hear the screaming?

JACK: What screaming?

CALLIE: Libby was screaming bloody murder.

JACK: I can sleep through anything.

LIBBY: Blood…the blood…

JACK: What the hang is up with her?

CALLIE: I don't know, but I wish she'd stop.

LIBBY: Statue of…somebody…gushing blood. Gerry?

CALLIE: Shades of Calpurnia's dream.

JACK: Huh?

CALLIE: Julius Caesar's wife…her nightmare, on the eve of his assassination. She saw Caesar's statue spurting blood like a fountain.

ALENA: Not exactly. That's what Shakespeare put in his play. She did dream of Casear lying stabbed in her arms. She begged him not to go to the Senate.

JACK: I can just hear her now "He never listened!"

GERALD: *(Notices the whiteboard.)* What the…! *(Grabs a lantern, holds it up to the whiteboard.)* Who rubbed out my notes? Who put this here?

ALENA: "*Iacta alea est.*" Speak of Caesar, and his words appear.

GERALD: Who did this?

JACK: Don't look at me. I was snoozing, big time.

GERALD: Those were very important notes—a detailed outline for my book! *(To ALENA.)* Was it you? Couldn't resist the opportunity to undercut me, again?

ALENA: I won't even dignify that with a response.

CALLIE: Some bad blood between you two?

ALENA: Back in school, Gerry and I were a tad competitive.

GERALD: "A tad"? We compared marks after every exam, every paper.

ALENA: I always won. It's true. And he's under the mistaken impression that I nicked his undergrad thesis idea.

GERALD: I'm not the least bit mistaken. You stole my ideas, used them to get the prof I wanted for an advisor.

ALENA: Ancient history.

JACK: *(Indicates whiteboard.)* Wasn't that what Caesar said before crossing the Rubicon?

GERALD: You actually remember something I taught you?

JACK: I don't remember a whole lot, but it's a cool saying. *(Mimes blowing on and rolling dice.)* "The die is cast."

CALLIE: Is this somebody's idea of a joke…a riddle?

JACK: One of the ladies could be thinking of making a play for you, Mr. G. *(Sultry voice.)* "The die is cast."

CALLIE: Caesar said it before launching a war. I take it as a threat.

JACK: Come on!

CALLIE: Somebody skulking around, writing in the colour of blood, in the middle of the night, as we all slept?

JACK: Oooh, somebody sneaking around, writing stuff in Latin. Call the cops. *(Portrays a police officer on the phone.)* "Ohhhh, they used a red marker? Hang tight, we're sending in the SWAT team."

GERALD: Speaking of which—it's missing. My red marker.

JACK: Uh oh. I'm thinking that's his prize possession.

LIBBY: Burning with rage. Whoever wrote that.

JACK: Maybe it was you.

GERALD: Me?

JACK: You're kind of an angry guy.

GERALD: What?!

JACK: Maybe this is how you get your jollies, creeping out your guests.

GERALD: Guests? Guests are people whose company you enjoy, who visit when invited. You are a bunch of imbeciles who decided to hop in your cars during the snowstorm of the century, and who I brought into my home out of the goodness of my heart!

JACK: Sounds like "burning with rage" to me.

GERALD: Somebody muzzle him, or he's going out in the snow!

CALLIE: Like anybody would get in the way of that.

GERALD: Nobody sleeps until we get to the bottom of this.

JACK: Negatory.

GERALD: Make yourself some coffee.

JACK: For a smart guy, you're pretty dumb. Remember the bazillion times you tried this back in school? "Everybody stays for detention 'til we find out who put 'Mr. G. is an A-hole' on the board." You just end up punishing the innocent people, and the badass never spills. By the way, it was always me. *(Big grin.)*

GERALD: Tell me something I don't know. *(Beat.)* Why don't we start with who even has the capacity to write this? Obviously I'm on the list; so is Alena.

ALENA: And Callie, perhaps?

CALLIE: My Latin isn't great; but everybody knows that phrase.

GERALD: *(Indicates LIBBY and JACK.)* They're both former students. My first year teaching; and my last.

LIBBY: I have trouble remembering what I had for breakfast, let alone what I took in Latin forty years ago.

JACK: *(To LIBBY.)* Was he a hard-ass back then too?

LIBBY: Worse. I hear he mellowed with age.

ALENA: Why don't we pack it in until morning?

CALLIE: No. We need an explanation. Especially after Libby's dream.

GERALD: What does that have to do with anything?

CALLIE: I'm guessing it's another sign all is not well.

GERALD: Not the psychic garbage again.

CALLIE: This from a guy who sets a place at his table for a lar. That's why that chair is off limits, right?

JACK: Hello? No internet, no Google. What's a "lar"?

ALENA: A family god. It can be the spirit of an ancestor, or one of the great gods. Traditionally you set aside a chair for the lar.

GERALD: It's just a quaint custom.

ALENA: You tore a strip off him over it.

GERALD: I'm a creature of habit, alright? One of the hazards of living alone.

CALLIE: Who is your lar?

ALENA: I bet it's Apollo, isn't it? You always were enthralled by Apollo, and terrified of your Dionysian side.

JACK: Wah, wah, wah, alert, alert big brains talking in code, again!

ALENA: Apollo is the god of the sun, wisdom, rationality; Dionysus rules over the night, intuition, dark passions, madness.

JACK: I'm thinking Dionysus is the god of whiteouts.

ALENA: That's actually quite astute. The goal is to strike a balance between the Apollonian and Dionysian; Gerry was never very good at that.

CALLIE: You can read him like a book. Did you two date?

GERALD: No.

CALLIE: *(To ALENA.)* You don't look so sure.

ALENA: We went out once or twice. We were never a couple.

CALLIE: Who broke it off?

ALENA: I believe it was mutual.

LIBBY: Oh honey, it's never mutual.

ALENA: There was no chemistry. We were better off as friends.

JACK: Ah-ha. You broke his heart into itty bitty pieces. He's been pining for you all these years.

GERALD: Don't be ridiculous!

CALLIE: *(To LIBBY.)* Did you and Gerald date?

GERALD: I was her teacher.

CALLIE: Answer the question.

ALENA: You're both turning beet red.

CALLIE: Your first year teaching; you two would've been pretty close in age.

JACK: Mister G., you dog!

GERALD: It's nobody's business.

CALLIE: Anything to add?

LIBBY: No.

JACK: You bastard; you broke her heart.

GERALD: This subject is closed.

JACK: Heh, you started it.

GERALD: I said enough!

JACK: *(Ferociously.)* Get out of my face!

*GERALD backs away.*

CALLIE: Whoa.

LIBBY: *(Indicates ALENA.)* If you want to know the truth he left me for her.

CALLIE: You've got to be kidding!

JACK: *(To CALLIE.)* You ever dated Gerry? Everybody else has.

CALLIE: Never had the pleasure. You?

JACK: I thought about it; he's a looker. *(Beat.)* This is too much fun, but I'm going for firewood—we're low. *(Grabs a lantern, gets his coat, exits into mud room.)*

*LIBBY is struck by another spell.*

ALENA: *(To LIBBY.)* Are you alright?

JACK: *(Enters, in a panic.)* Holy cripes!

GERALD: What?

JACK: Mrs. Sturgeon!

ALENA: What about her?

GERALD: Spit it out, man.

JACK: She ain't out there.

GERALD: What do you mean? *(Grabs lantern from JACK, peers into mud room.)*

JACK: Do I have to frickin' spell it out for you? She's gone, blanket and all!

ALENA: Writing cryptic messages is one thing, but moving a body? This is creepy.

GERALD: Whoever is behind all of this…is going to be very, very sorry.

CALLIE: Maybe the whiteouts will stop and we can all just be on our way.

LIBBY: Four days.

ALENA: Sorry?

LIBBY: It just come to me. The whiteouts…they're going to last for four more days…and the blood…it's coming…it's coming.

## Scene 4 – Past Loves Revisited

*The wind shrieks.*

*Morning. The whiteboard is closed.*

*A distracted GERALD attempts to read a book.*

*JACK stares out of the window while making coffee. Heats water in a kettle on the wood stove, pours through filter directly into his cup.*

*CALLIE reads a book, observes the others.*

*LIBBY checks the phone to see if service has been restored; no such luck. She takes a cup of tea, paper and pen, sits away from the others and writes a letter.*

JACK: Will you stop!

GERALD: Who are you talking to?

JACK: The snow.

GERALD: That's productive.

JACK: Makes me feel better.

ALENA: *(Enters from hallway, carrying a pot.)* I feel almost human again. Although there's only so much you can do without electricity and a toothbrush.

JACK: Gerry would probably let you use his toothbrush; you two have swapped spit before.

ALENA: Mrs. Sturgeon didn't happen to turn up?

JACK: Yeah. Turns out she just went for Chinese.

CALLIE: This is probably really stupid but…is it possible she wasn't dead?

GERALD: No. She didn't walk off. Somebody moved her. I've combed every inch of this place…somebody must've dumped her outside. She was light as a feather—anybody could've done it.

CALLIE: But why?

JACK: Somebody is messing with our heads.

ALENA: But, why? *(To GERALD.)* I can't get over all of us knowing you, or knowing of you.

GERALD: Life in a small town.

JACK: Hilarious a couple weeks ago, guy goes to stick up the gas station and the lady goes, "Colton, get the bleep out of here or I'll call your mother!"

CALLIE: Maybe the Fates brought us together, for some reason. I've been thinking about what was in your notebook…"one life-thread is cut"—that could be Mrs. Sturgeon. "Five more intertwine"—there's five of us.

GERALD: *(Dismissively.)* Hocus pocus.

ALENA: Speaking of the Fates, why don't you tell us about your book?

JACK: Yeah, everybody walks around saying "it was fate" and stuff; what's it all about?

ALENA: The Fates are goddesses, very powerful goddesses. None of the other gods can over-rule them. There's three of them—

GERALD: —They're sisters. Nona spins the thread of life, Decuma decides the length, and Morta cuts, at the moment of death.

CALLIE: I've never really delved into them; did the Ancient Romans believe in total predestination?

ALENA: No—

GERALD: —They believed in a combination of destiny and free will. Before you're born, the Fates decide the length of your life, how and when you'll die.

ALENA: And they draw lots, to randomly allocate the amount of good and evil that will happen to you in your life.

GERALD: But this is essential; your fate isn't completely random...you can amplify the evil due to you, through your own folly.

JACK: So the Fates decided yesterday Mrs. Sturgeon's number was up, and it was going to be a whiteout that got her?

ALENA: They could've determined that before she was even born, or—

GERALD: —Or she was fated to die peacefully in her sleep, but due to her own folly, the Fates arranged a less pleasant demise.

LIBBY: "Folly"? Mrs. Sturgeon?

GERALD: We know at the very least she had an unhealthy obsession with shopping.

CALLIE: So what slant are you taking, in your book?

GERALD: *(Glares at ALENA.)* Experience has taught me to keep my ideas close to the vest.

*JACK looks for a place to put his mug on the coffee table, plunks it on top of a book.*

*(Grabs JACK's mug.)* Van Bakel! What are you doing!?

JACK: What?!

GERALD: *(Holds up book.)* This is not a coaster!

CALLIE: *(To GERALD.)* He doesn't get it. To him it's just an object.

JACK: You do know I'm standing right here?

GERALD: *(Gets JACK a coaster.)* Books are…sacred, in this house.

CALLIE: Don't bother. Van Bakel. Dutch. You can tell them a mile away, but you can't tell them much.

JACK: Har, har, har. So you moved away to the city, act all sophisticated, but you're still a redneck, a hundred percent.

CALLIE: Whoa, I touched a nerve. Thought you would've laughed that off, come back with something like, "yeah I'm Dutch and you're jealous".

JACK: What's your last name? How be I cut up your background, see how you like it?

ALENA: *(Eureka.)* Van Bakel. Where is your farm, exactly? You're not attached to the lawsuit?

JACK: What lawsuit? Oh that lawsuit, by a bunch of city slicker cottagers, who looooove the country and their 'beloved Lake Huron', so long as the animals are trained not to shit on weekends, and all summer.

ALENA: No, we just object to it being generated on an industrial scale.

GERALD: House rule: politics and religion are fine, but no discussing nutrient management.

JACK: That's actually pretty funny, Mr. G.

ALENA: Sounds like you were two steps ahead of me. How soon after we arrived did you realize who I am?

JACK: Didn't take long.

LIBBY: Your farm isn't anywhere near the lake.

JACK: Not the home farm, but we partnered up on an operation over there.

ALENA: Sounds like you're over-extended. The high dollar is killing you, you're losing money on every pig.

JACK: The pork business is up and down like a toilet seat. Always has been, always will be.

ALENA: Now you've got to pay to defend yourselves in court. We hear some of you are at the breaking point.

JACK: We'll break you.

ALENA: Sounds like a threat.

GERALD: I wouldn't take his threats lightly.

JACK: I know what you're talking about; that was self-defence.

GERALD: You beat two men to within an inch of their lives.

JACK: I'm the nicest guy you'll ever meet, unless you mess with me.

CALLIE: Does her lawsuit qualify as "messing" with you?

JACK: I'm talking about being attacked, like in a fight. Somebody comes at me right now, hundred per cent, I'll beat him down, mash him to a pulp.

ALENA: That's fairly violent.

JACK: Believe me, if I wanted to have it out with you, I wouldn't sneak around in the dark, or muck around with a body.

CALLIE: Maybe you're just getting warmed up.

JACK: Who asked you? We don't even know your last name.

LIBBY: Your aunt who died—that wouldn't be Velma Rutledge? You sure look like a Rutledge.

GERALD: Yes, she does.

CALLIE: Yeah, that's right.

LIBBY: Velma had a hard life. Your uncle wasn't a nice man. Sorry.

CALLIE: Don't apologise. He was an ignorant prick.

GERALD: I taught Hal. Or tried.

JACK: Hal Rutledge… I heard of him. My dad said he used his wife and kids as punching bags. One time my dad tried to pass him, and Hal ran my dad right off the road.

GERALD: Volatile, violent, and dumb as a post. Somebody asked who was my worst student ever…well Hal managed to fail History not once, but twice.

LIBBY: He sure wasn't fond of you. Without passing

History, he never could get his Grade Twelve.

ALENA: *(To CALLIE.)* Gerry's name must've been mud in your family.

CALLIE: Gerry didn't do Uncle Hal any favours. But, the surprise would've been if he'd actually got his high school diploma.

GERALD: Amen.

JACK: You called Huron County "godforsaken", said you had a hard time growing up around here. Your uncle have anything to do with that?

CALLIE: My parents kept us clear of him. But my family was dysfunctional enough all on its own.

JACK: They say ninety-two per cent of families are dysfunctional; and nobody's ever met the other eight per cent.

GERALD: *(Exasperated.)* And around and around we go… I'm going to get dressed.

ALENA: *(Indicates GERALD and JACK.)* But you two are so adorable in your matching p-js.

*GERALD exits down hallway.*

*ALENA goes over to LIBBY.*

You're pretty quiet over here. What are you up to?

LIBBY: Just writing a letter, to my family.

JACK: Say hey to Trisha for me.

LIBBY: Fat chance. *(To ALENA.)* It's pretty silly.

ALENA: No.

LIBBY: I'm just not used to… not being able to talk to them. *(Tucks letter away.)*

ALENA: I've been wanting to tell you when I dated Gerald, I had no idea he was involved with somebody else.

LIBBY: He taught for a year right out of high school. You could do that back then.

ALENA: I know.

LIBBY: We fell for each other, but then he went off to university and met you. You were the kind of woman he wanted, not little old me.

ALENA: Don't say that. Seems like things turned out alright for you. The truth is I envy you.

LIBBY: That'd be the day.

ALENA: Honestly. I'm the last person my daughter would turn to if she broke up with her boyfriend.

LIBBY: Really?

GERALD: *(Enters.)* I'm guessing she never had time for her kids. Her career comes first, ahead of everything and everyone.

ALENA: A price must be paid for excellence.

GERALD: And you'd fork over anything, including your soul.

ALENA: You don't know me.

GERALD: I know you well. To this day I'm shocked at what you offered up, to keep me quiet, about stealing my ideas.

JACK: *(Suggestively.)* Are we talking about what I think we're talking about?

ALENA: Gerry, Gerry, Gerry. Are you so envious of my career that you have to blame me for yours never getting off the ground?

LIBBY: He wanted to be a professor and write books. He wasn't going to end up back here, teaching in "the sticks".

GERALD: I was young and arrogant. I changed; my goals changed. *(Indicating ALENA.)* She, for one, turned me off the cut-throat world of academia.

LIBBY: When you moved back…the way you looked at me…seemed like you were pretty sorry you broke things off.

ALENA: Don't tell me I'm responsible that, too? Perhaps I'm somehow to blame for Jack and Trisha breaking up?

CALLIE: *(To LIBBY.)* Why did they break up? Did he ever hit her?

JACK: No! I loved Trisha to bits; I wanted to marry her. But she knew her mom was dead set against me.

CALLIE: Why was that? *(Beat.)* Ah! You foresaw something.

JACK: That's what you had against me—one of your stupid friggin' dreams?!

Don't tell me you saw me hurting her, because that'd be a crock!!

*CALLIE grabs Libby's letter.*

LIBBY: Heh, give that back!

CALLIE: "If I never see you again…"!

LIBBY: That's private! *(Grabs letter back.)*

CALLIE: What do you know!?

*A tearful LIBBY rushes down the hall.*

JACK: You people are frickin' losing it!

ALENA: No… I've got a pit in my stomach. *Cavet anguis in herba.*

GERALD: There's no snake in the grass.

ALENA: There certainly is. It's like in the summer, when that psycho was on the loose. I couldn't eat, couldn't sleep—I had to head back to London.

JACK: *(Laughs.)* I'm not being a jerk. It's just the first I heard of somebody leaving here for the city to feel safe; it's usually the other way around.

ALENA: I say if we're still stuck here tonight, we sleep in shifts, keep watch.

CALLIE: Great idea.

JACK: Come on!

CALLIE: Maybe you're down on the concept because it'll mess up your plans.

JACK: I'm busted. Tonight, while you were sleeping, I was going write "kick me" in purple marker on all your left butt cheeks. *(Beat.)* OK, to show I'm a team player, I'll be a sub. Any of you are on watch and need a break, give me an elbow.

CALLIE: If anybody takes him up on that, wake me up too; I don't want to sleep on his watch.

JACK: Heh, then we'll end up on watch together. Ahhh, I'm getting the warm and fuzzies all over.

GERALD: These two might strangle each other in broad daylight.

ALENA: *Mala avi.* A bad omen, to speak of murder.

*Blackout.*

## Scene 5 – A Murder and an Exit

*The wind shrieks.*

*Total black.*

*Sound of a chair being knocked over, thumping to the floor.*

JACK: Ah!!

CALLIE: What was that?!

JACK: Damn it!!

GERALD: The light!?

*GERALD clicks on the lantern near him. He stands, wrapped in blankets—he has been sitting on his chair at the kitchen table.*

*CALLIE sits on another kitchen chair, wrapped in blankets.*

*JACK hops on one foot, clutching his other foot with one hand. At his feet is the special kitchen chair for GERALD's lar.*

*LIBBY sits up in an armchair, wrapped in blankets. She clicks on a lantern near her.*

*The couch has been slept on, but nobody is there.*

*The door to the hallway is shut.*

*Unnoticed by all, written in large, red letters on the whiteboard is "Mors omnibus parata est."*

JACK: Agh!! Stubbed my toe. How come all the frickin' lights were off?

GERALD: I left mine on; I don't know how it got turned off.

JACK: You were on watch?

GERALD: I must've drifted off.

CALLIE: Me too.

JACK: Nice work, sentries.

CALLIE: What were you doing prowling around?

JACK: I have to pee. Is that allowed?

CALLIE: The washroom is that way.

JACK: It was pitch black. I didn't know which way was up.

LIBBY: Where's Alena?

CALLIE: Yeah. *(Exits down hall, offstage knocks on washroom door.)* Anybody home? *(Enters.)* She's not in the washroom.

GERALD: The bedrooms?

JACK: Why would she be back there?

CALLIE: Just go check.

*JACK takes a lantern, exits down hallway.*

JACK: *(Offstage.)* Heh, professor?! Wakey, wakey! You in here? *(Enters.)* Nope.

GERALD: Maybe she went for firewood.

LIBBY: Alone?

GERALD: Her coat is gone. *(Grabs his coat and a lantern, exits into mud room.)*

*JACK holds open the door to the mud room.*

*Offstage sound of the door to the garage opening.*

*(Offstage.)* Alena?

LIBBY: Dear God, let her be alright.

CALLIE: Yeah.

GERALD: *(Offstage.)* Alena?! Oh no! Oh… God!

JACK: What?!

*JACK exits into mud room.*

*CALLIE and LIBBY hold open the door to the mud room.*

CALLIE: What's going on?! Is she OK?!

*JACK enters, stumbling, in shock.*

GERALD: *(Offstage, frantic.)* Help! Help me! Get back here!!

CALLIE: Jack!?

JACK: She's… she's dead.

LIBBY: No!

*CALLIE exits to mud room, and the garage.*

CALLIE: *(Offstage, screams.)* Ahhh!!!

*CALLIE enters, horrified.*

LIBBY: How…? What happened?

JACK: Sorry?

LIBBY: What happened to her?

JACK: Back of her head…all caved in.

LIBBY: Oh Lord!

JACK: Axe…beside her. All covered in…blood…hair…

CALLIE: Oh God. *(Gags.)*

LIBBY: I don't understand.

JACK: Somebody killed her. Somebody effin' killed her!

LIBBY: No!

JACK: Mr. G. is flipping out.

*LIBBY grabs a blanket, exits into mud room.*

CALLIE: How could anybody…?

JACK: Why didn't I listen? Thought somebody was just messing with us.

CALLIE: *(Breaks into tears.)* What are we going to do?

JACK: Oh man, oh man…

*Offstage, sound of door closing.*

*LIBBY leads in a shocked GERALD. She no longer has the blanket.*

GERALD: Who did this? Who!? You better pray… Was it you?! I'll tear you apart!

JACK: No, Gerry! No! I swear! I'd never…

GERALD: Who, then?! Who!? *(Beat.)* Who's that?!

JACK: Where?! Shit!

GERALD: There!! On the floor!!

JACK: It's…it's just a sleeping bag! See?!

CALLIE: He nearly gave me a heart attack.

GERALD: *(Reacts to something in his peripheral vision.)* Ahh!!!

LIBBY: What?!

JACK: Geez! What the hell!?

GERALD: Get out of here. All of you.

JACK: Hold your horses.

GERALD: I bring you into my home…give you shelter, food…

JACK: Just calm down, and think!

GERALD: *(Grabs all of their coats, hurls them on the floor.)* Get out!

JACK: It's a crying shame about Alena but…

GERALD: Shut your mouth! Get out! Get the hell out!

JACK: You want to kill us? Because that's what you're talking about. You don't know any of us did… that…let alone all three of us. You couldn't leave a dead body out in that weather!

*Beat.*

GERALD: Damn it all!!

*LIBBY points to the whiteboard.*

*Mors omnibus parata est*. Death…has been prepared for all.

LIBBY: Oh God.

*CALLIE scrambles into her coat and boots.*

JACK: What do you think you're doing?

CALLIE: Stay away from me!

JACK: Give your head a shake.

CALLIE: I'm not staying here waiting to be… *(Grabs a lantern.)*

GERALD: No.

CALLIE: You've got two more. You can't send me out in the pitch dark, in whiteouts, with nothing.

JACK: It's suicide, either way. Maybe we shouldn't let her go anyway. What if she's the one who…?

CALLIE: I'm not! And I'm not staying here! No way!

LIBBY: This isn't happening.

JACK: This from the one who freakin' predicted it.

CALLIE: I'm leaving, with or without a light.

GERALD: *(Gives the flashlight to CALLIE.)* Closest neighbours are north, this side of the road. Gary and Steph. Send help if you can.

CALLIE: Two of you good luck. The other…rot in hell! *(Exits.)*

*Offstage in mud room wind howls louder, then door to outside slams shut.*

GERALD: She is as good as dead.

JACK: We got to settle down, think.

LIBBY: Poor, poor Alena.

JACK: We got bigger fish to fry.

GERALD: What!? A brilliant woman lies…killed…another is on her way to freeze to death…what could possibly…?

JACK: The writing is on the wall. Death has been prepared for all. Right quick, we got to figure this out; our lives depend on it.

*The lights close in on a frantic GERALD, who hears the Fates speaking.*

NONA: Blood has been spilled:

DECUMA: There will be more still

MORTA: I have more and more graves to fill

*Blackout.*

# Act II

## Scene 1 – The Fates Accuse

*The wind shrieks.*

*Fifteen minutes has passed.*

*GERALD sits still.*

*LIBBY cries and dabs at her eyes with tissues.*

*JACK paces and devours a box of crackers.*

JACK: Think, think, think. Maybe the killer dropped something, or...blood spatter...no way the killer could've done what they done without blood getting on them. And dad says I'm wasting my time watching all them crime scene shows!

LIBBY: How can you eat?

JACK: When I'm stressed, I eat. What was she doing out there? She was nervous as hell; no way she'd go out to the garage alone. Maybe the killer lured her out there somehow?

LIBBY: Asked her for help, to get the firewood, maybe?

JACK: That would make you the killer; me or Gerald wouldn't need help.

GERALD: "Neither Gerald nor I would need help."

JACK: You're cutting up my grammar? Killer, whoever

you are, just shoot me: now! *(Beat, to LIBBY.)* I got to tell you something. You don't want to hear this, but I love Trisha, more than ever.

LIBBY: Save it.

JACK: I'm bound and bent I'm going to make it out of here, and the first thing I'm going to do is beg her to take me back.

LIBBY: She'll tell you to go pound salt.

JACK: She is the only one who never asked me to act different. My mom and dad, brothers and sisters, teachers, every other girlfriend I ever had…"now in front of these people don't say this…and don't joke about that…and don't act the way you usually act…" She is the only one, ever. It's got to be New Year's. She loves New Year's. So I got two days. By your forecast, the whiteouts are supposed to stop by then, right?

GERALD: Why did I ever look out that window?

*Sound of door to outside in mud room opening, then slamming shut.*

JACK: What the…?! *(Quietly.)* Maybe we been barking up the wrong tree; maybe it's not one of us at all.

*JACK and GERALD grab lanterns, wield them like weapons.*

*The door to the mud room flies open and… CALLIE enters, shivering uncontrollably.*

LIBBY: Callie!

*JACK moves to help CALLIE.*

*CALLIE rebuffs JACK, stumbles over to the wood stove.*

JACK: Here, have a blanket.

*CALLIE snatches the blanket, drapes it around herself.*

JACK: You're welcome. Hate to say "I told you so"...

CALLIE: Then don't! I ended up on my hands and knees, tracing my footprints back...my fast-disappearing footprints.

JACK: Sorry to cut the reunion short, but I'm headed out to the garage, to look for clues. Anybody want to come?

CALLIE: *(To LIBBY, indicates GERALD.)* Don't leave me alone with him.

JACK: *(Grabs his coat.)* Heh, what's all over my stuff?

GERALD: Looks like dried blood. A lot of dried blood.

CALLIE: Guess you found a clue; a really good one.

GERALD: So it was you!

JACK: No! Don't look at me like that. The killer must've put on my stuff, to keep their's clean, make me look guilty.

CALLIE: Alena told me she was the lynch-pin in the lawsuit. Looks like you saved your family and friends from financial ruin.

JACK: I'm not saying I'd never kill nobody. In self defence, in a war—sure. But over money? Never.

LIBBY: I think it's high time I tell why I was against him and Trisha...I had the same dream, many a time. *(Cries.)* Of him, holding an axe, way up high over his head, face all red and angry.

JACK: Bullshit!

LIBBY: I could never see who he was going to hit, but I could tell it was a woman.

CALLIE: You wait until now to tell us this?

LIBBY: My dreams don't work like that...they don't usually show exactly what's going to happen.

JACK: Come on! You come out with a dream about me axe-murdering somebody after somebody shows up axe-murdered?

LIBBY: It's true; I swear.

JACK: OK now I'm thinking it's you. My money was on Mr. G., but after this little b.s. act... Did you have to get even with Alena for stealing him away: from you?

LIBBY: No. I'd never...

CALLIE: *(To JACK.)* Nice try. Everything points to you.

JACK: Think what you like. I'm going to find some real evidence.

GERALD: *(Points to JACK's coat.)* Leave that. That's evidence.

JACK: Crap. *(Takes off his boots and coat.)* Try not to miss me too much. *(Exits.)*

CALLIE: It's got to be him. What can we do? Lock him out there?

GERALD: Wood doors; the axe is still out there.

CALLIE: I don't want to die.

GERALD: *(Fetches three large knives from the kitchen.)* There're three of us.

*CALLIE accepts a knife.*

LIBBY: *(Refuses a knife.)* I couldn't.

GERALD: *(Sets down a knife near her.)* You might change your mind.

CALLIE: Ahhh! I'm chilled to the bone!

LIBBY: It must've been hell out there.

CALLIE: Even worse than in here. If somebody is after you, at least you've got a fighting chance. Out there blind, freezing…it's actually claustrophobic; the world ends right here, an inch in front of your face…like you're entombed.

LIBBY: Thank goodness you found your way back.

CALLIE: Right back to square one: a precipice in front of me, wolves behind.

GERALD: Like you say at least you can fight a wolf.

*GERALD sees something in the window, panics, drops his knife, hides his eyes.*

*LIBBY sees something also and is startled.*

CALLIE: What?! What is it?

LIBBY: *(To GERALD.)* You see them?

CALLIE: See who?! What are you talking about?!

GERALD: I'm losing my mind.

LIBBY: No, you're not.

GERALD: "Who the gods wish to destroy, they first make mad".

LIBBY: You're not nuts. They're gone now.

*GERALD peeks.*

CALLIE: Who did you see?

LIBBY: Three old, old women.

GERALD: You really saw them?

LIBBY: In the window. With great, big hoods.

GERALD: Was sure my mind was…playing tricks on me… again.

LIBBY: You're just a bit of a psychic, like I always told you. Not that you ever listened to me. You know who they were.

GERALD: Fata. The Fates.

CALLIE: You saw them?! What did they want? Did they say anything?

GERALD: They just stared, with those terrible, damning eyes, as if to say, "you've amplified the evil due to you, through your own folly."

LIBBY: You're not the only one they were staring at.

JACK: *(Enters, looking shaken.)* Zippo. No hairs, nothing dropped. Well there's bloody footprints, my boots, but nothing to say who was wearing them.

CALLIE: No clues found by the prime suspect…what a shocker.

JACK: Heh, what's with the knives? *(Beat.)* OK, OK, look, it could be any of us. I say we take a shot at getting inside the head of the killer. Maybe whoever it is just likes offing people, so this will be pretty useless, but…let's say we're dealing with a person an axe to grind…sorry, poor choice of words… OK Mr. G., I got to ask this whole jealousy thing with Alena…how bad was it?

GERALD: I'm in no mood for this.

CALLIE: Alena lived your dream, while you toiled in obscurity. Why were you so hard on your students? Sign of a bitter man.

JACK: Who died and left you Head of Questions? This is my idea.

CALLIE: Fine, go ahead.

JACK: So, Mister G., were you bitter?

CALLIE: Great question.

JACK: Watch, and learn.

GERALD: She wasn't my favourite person. But I know all too well I'm to blame for my own failures. *(Gestures toward garage.)* And I could never, ever do…that… to anybody.

JACK: I don't buy it. It was him. A hundred percent.

CALLIE: *(To LIBBY.)* What about the split, between you two? How did things end?

LIBBY: Honestly? It was terrible. I thought we were good together. I thought we were in love.

GERALD: We were.

LIBBY: So why end it? Forty years later, and I still don't know. I only got the lame crap you handed me, and my best guess.

CALLIE: What's your—

JACK: —Nuh-uh-uh! What's your best guess?

LIBBY: I wasn't good enough for him. He wanted somebody like Alena, somebody impressive. One time we were out for a walk, and I told him, "I want a normal life. I want a family, good friends, a nice home—an ordinary life." *(To GERALD.)* You looked at me like I had two heads.

GERALD: I was a fool. A young, arrogant ass.

CALLIE: *(To LIBBY.)* So you're stranded here, all of those old feelings get stirred…

JACK: *(To CALLIE.)* You're doing it again. *(To LIBBY.)* So you're stranded here and you see the chickee-poo he dumped you for, and your blood starts a-boiling. Am I right, or am I right?

LIBBY: I've got a great life, the life I always wanted. If anybody is bitter, it's him.

GERALD: My heart told me to never let you go. My head said, we were just too different. Do you know how often I've wished I'd gone with my heart?

JACK: You went with Apollo, gave Dionysus the finger; what else is new?

CALLIE: *(Eureka, to LIBBY.)* Did he get you pregnant?

JACK: Ooooh, killer question. I would've thought of that.

CALLIE: Did he?

GERALD: Don't tell me…

LIBBY: This is a conversation for me and Gerry.

JACK: What are you going to do—go for a latte?

GERALD: If I have a child in this world and don't know about it…

JACK: *(Blanches.)* Holy crap.

CALLIE: What?

JACK: I'm adopted. And I got no idea who my bio parents are. Mom? Dad? Oh God that would make Trisha my… *(Fit of revulsion.)* No wonder you were against her and me…

CALLIE: Hello?! She just said all of this happened forty years ago. And you're…mid-twenties?

JACK: Good point. Whew. Man, that would've been serious.

GERALD: Libby.

LIBBY: I miscarried, OK? There, now you know. Otherwise I would've told you.

JACK: Man, I was so hoping there was a love child. *(Beat.)* OK so it's not Mr. G.; it's her. She hates him for dumping her and leaving her preggers. She hated Alena for stealing him away. I already know she hates my guts. Then I go and tell her I'm going to make another play for Trisha. Talk about waving a red flag in front of a bull; holy smokers!

LIBBY: Alena was bankrupting your family. Gerald treated you like dirt. Girlie here dared insult your Dutch heritage -- and funny enough, you might not have a drop of Dutch blood in you. In your mind I mucked up your only chance at happiness, with Trisha. Not to mention, you're the one with blood all over your stuff.

JACK: Damn. It's me. A hundred per cent. Wait a minute! I know it's not me. *(To CALLIE.)* What about you? Maybe your aunt and cousins weren't the only ones your mean uncle lit into…and you blame Mr. G.

CALLIE: So why go after Alena?

JACK: You got a lot of nerve; even when you're supposed to be answering a question, you ask questions! *(Beat.)* Why Alena? I'll tell you why. You looked fit to be tied, after she pointed out you're taking your sweet time getting your PhD. And, if you're after Mr. G., you can't leave any witnesses.

CALLIE: Was there a question in there?

JACK: Oh yeah. Uh…what do you have to say about that?

CALLIE: I almost died trying to get away from here.

JACK: Valid.

GERALD: This is work; this is labour.

LIBBY: And work tires you out. Sooner or later, we're going to have to sleep again.

## Scene 2 – Libby Focuses Her Powers

*The wind shrieks.*

*The whiteboard is blank.*

*GERALD and LIBBY sit near each other, and CALLIE is off on her own.*

*JACK devours cookies, takes a kettle off the wood stove, pours hot water through a filter full of coffee grounds into his mug, chugs it, starts making another mug.*

*JACK also uses a can opener to open canned food (soups, veggies, sauces). He empties the contents into plastic containers to store in the fridge. Then he rinses out the cans. He stops when he has about a dozen empty cans at his disposal.*

JACK: I'm not sleeping until next year. I'm gonna be bright-eyed and bushy tailed for the duration. Alert, alive, enthusiastic. Nobody's sneaking up on me, catching me with my guard down, no, no, no. I'm super-duper-extra awake. I could give a class on awake-icity.

GERALD: It's not the killer he needs to worry about; he is going to O.D. on caffeine.

JACK: I heard that, with my super-hearing. It's so good, I can hear all of your hearts beating from here. Well, except Callie. If she had a heart, I'd hear it. *(Beat.)* Aw, come on, where happened to your fire?

GERALD: What are you doing with my food?

JACK: Nothing. It's the cans I want.

GERALD: What for?

JACK: That's for me to know, and you to find out.

GERALD: Tell me, or stop.

JACK: Let's just say if I do happen to nod off tonight, ain't nobody going to be sneaking up on me.

LIBBY: What happened to your fire?

GERALD: Sorry?

LIBBY: All your big dreams? *(Indicates CALLIE.)* You were like her and Alena this place was too small for you.

JACK: Is this a "let's-try-and- trip-up-the-killer" kind of thing, or are you just being nosey? Or are you trying to make him feel like crap? Which is OK too.

LIBBY: Just curious.

CALLIE: The usual. Fear. Complacency.

GERALD: What do you know about my life?

CALLIE: You failed, according to the bar you set for yourself.

GERALD: I adjusted the bar.

CALLIE: Translation: you learned to rationalize, lie to yourself.

JACK: *(To CALLIE.)* What have you ever done?

GERALD: Probably not much; most accomplished people I've met are much more gracious. *(Beat, to LIBBY.)* Didn't you know way back when, what would become of me? Apparently you can see the future.

LIBBY: I'm always cloudiest about my own life, and the

people closest to me. But I thought you were a doer. If I remember right, that's one of the things you admired most about the Romans: they got things done.

GERALD: I frittered my life away. Folly. My life is rife with folly.

CALLIE: *(To LIBBY.)* You said the Fates stared at you too. What folly are you guilty of?

JACK: Huh? Did I miss something?

CALLIE: You were in the garage.

LIBBY: Gerry never got the life he wanted; I got mine, but not honestly. My husband was supposed to marry somebody else.

JACK: Chuck?

LIBBY: He was on the rebound when I met him, from his first love, who'd broken off their engagement. After me and Chuck got together, his ex had a change of heart, wanted Chuck back. He was torn. He made up his mind to go back to her. I couldn't stand being thrown over for another woman—again. So I did a terrible thing.

JACK: You murdered her!

LIBBY: No! I lied. And abused my "gift." I "saw" Chuck was supposed to be with the other gal, but I told him the opposite, that he was meant to marry me.

JACK: I'm thinking he knew you had an itty bitty conflict of interest.

LIBBY: I scared him, told him if he went back to her, there was no telling what could happen to her, so he'd wind up back with me.

CALLIE: No kidding, you're on the Fates' shit list. You screwed with their plans for three people, at least.

LIBBY: The other gal is still alive; never married. If I don't make it out of here, her and Chuck just might end up—

GERALD: —Don't talk like that.

JACK: Everybody still buying her dream about me with an axe? Just asking.

LIBBY: I told you that time with Chuck, that was the one and only time I ever did anything like that.

CALLIE: So what was Alena's folly? She must've done something to die like that. Pride? Excessive ambition? Dishonesty?

GERALD: How about, "D", all of the above.

JACK: Lib, I been thinking…you ever tried to…focus your powers?

LIBBY: My "powers?"

JACK: You're kind of hit and miss, and even the good stuff you come up with isn't real specific. But, say we burn incense or chant, or do tai chi or some crap like that, and you really bear down, try and come up with something like, "watch out for Gerald, he's got a loaded forty-five in the desk drawer." Worth a shot?

LIBBY: No.

CALLIE: *(Indicates GERALD and LIBBY.)* You two never should've split up; you're perfect for each other.

LIBBY: What's that supposed to mean?

CALLIE: Complacency. You've got this remarkable gift and you've never tried to develop it?

LIBBY: It works fine, without mucking with it.

CALLIE: Complacency.

LIBY: You're so quick to judge other people. And so harsh.

JACK: *(To LIBBY, indicating CALLIE.)* Don't mind her. She's scared, and it's making her even grumpier than usual—which is saying something. Why not give it a shot? We do we got to lose?

LIBBY: Fine. No incense, though; I hate the smell of that stuff.

*CALLIE goes to the kitchen, makes herself a coffee.*

JACK: *(To CALLIE.)* Hands off my cans.

LIBBY: Maybe I should try the lar chair?

GERALD: Certainly.

JACK: Yeah, move your ass, Apollo.

GERALD: Jack!

*LIBBY sits down, closes her eyes.*

CALLIE: I don't know what the point is.

JACK: Will you shush?

CALLIE: If she's the killer, she can just invent a bunch of stuff, throw suspicion on somebody else.

JACK: A minute ago you were ragging on her for doing nothing. Now you're ragging her for doing something. Shut it. *(Beat.)* Holy crap Lib, you're levitatin'. Kidding. Sorry, I'll zip it.

*LIBBY lets out a series of long, eerie moans.*

*JACK gives a grin and a thumbs-up to GERALD and CALLIE.*

*More moans from LIBBY.*

*LIBBY slumps over just is there is a loud bang, like a gunshot.*

*GERALD, CALLIE and JACK cry out.*

JACK: What the hell!?

GERALD: I think it was the stove… wood popping.

JACK: Excuse me while I go change my underpants.

GERALD: Libby? Are you alright?

*LIBBY stirs, tries to sit up, isn't strong enough.*

Just rest.

JACK: Looked like you were really getting in a groove there.

LIBBY: I saw a few things.

JACK: Great! Lay it on us.

LIBBY: Gerry…is the key to everything.

CALLIE: He's the killer?

LIBBY: Not necessarily.

JACK: Maybe he's an accomplice, or…the main target? I think we're getting somewhere! What else you got?

LIBBY: There's a spirit, behind all of this.

JACK: *(Terrified.)* Sweet Baby Jesus! Ghosts can kill people? They can just pop out of nowhere and start swinging an axe? That sucks! How do you fight that?

GERALD: Simmer down.

JACK: Simmer down!? There's an axe-murdering ghost on the loose!

LIBBY: No, no, the spirit is behind what's happening, at the root. It's a living person we got to worry about.

JACK: You sure? Because I can sort of deal with that. OK, maybe not the best idea ever, drinking all that coffee.

LIBBY: There are clues close by, but we can't see them. And…one of us gals is in the greatest danger now.

CALLIE: Which one?

LIBBY: I'm not sure.

JACK: Is that it?

LIBBY: Yeah.

JACK: Why don't we give her another go? Maybe you can get some more.

GERALD: She's completely drained.

LIBBY: Maybe later.

JACK: You sure?

CALLIE: What are you worried about? One of us is next on the list.

*Blackout.*

## Scene 3 – Another Murder, Another Exit

*The wind shrieks. Total black.*

*GERALD clicks on a lantern.*

*GERALD, JACK, and CALLIE are sitting up, wrapped in blankets.*

*JACK and CALLIE are asleep.*

*All around JACK on the floor are cans strung together with thread.*

*One chair is empty, with blankets draped over it.*

*The door to the hallway is ajar.*

*On the whiteboard in red marker is written: Acheruntis pabulum.*

*Unseen by GERALD, an inert figure lies on the couch covered by the same red blanket that was on the couch at the top of the play, the one GERALD used to wrap up Mrs. Sturgeon.*

*The globe is missing from GERALD's desk.*

*GERALD checks the whiteboard and notices the message.*

*He stands close, scrutinizing it.*

CALLIE: What are you doing?!

GERALD: Ah! Damn! You scared the life out of me!

CALLIE: Did you just write that?

GERALD: No! I fell asleep, again!

CALLIE: Same here.

GERALD: *(Notices figure on couch.)* Oh God!

CALLIE: Do you have two blankets like that?

*GERALD shakes his head "no".*

JACK: *(Wakes up.)* What's happening?

CALLIE: Mrs. Sturgeon is back.

JACK: No, seriously. Holy crap! *(Jumps up, sets off his own booby trap causing a great clatter; untangles himself with difficulty.)* Heh, where's Libby?

*ALL look at the figure on the couch.*

JACK: *(Calls down the hall.)* Libby? Oh Libby!?

GERALD: Oh no.

*JACK gathers his nerve, approaches the couch, whips off the blanket.*

*Suddenly the globe usually found on GERALD's desk rolls off the couch and bangs to the floor, startling JACK, CALLIE, and GERALD.*

*It is not a body on the couch at all, but pillows arranged to look like a body, and the globe which served as the head.*

CALLIE: What the hell?

JACK: Bugger!

GERALD: I'm losing my mind.

JACK: Heh, what's on the whiteboard?

GERALD: *Acheruntis pabulum.*

JACK: Huh?

GERALD: Food for Acheruns. One of the seven rivers that flows around Hell.

JACK: I don't get it.

GERALD: When you say somebody is food for Acheruns, you mean they're so awful, so vile, that they really, truly deserve to die.

CALLIE: We have to look for Libby.

JACK: Where?

CALLIE: The garage?

GERALD: I'll check the bedrooms.

*CALLIE and JACK grab lanterns and their coats, exit to mudroom.*

*GERALD gets a lantern, goes to the hall, pushes on door, it won't open fully.*

*He peeks in, recoils and drops his lantern—it clatters to the floor.*

*CALLIE and JACK enter on the run.*

JACK: What's the matter!? Mr. G.? *(Peeks in hallway, recoils.)* Ah, no!

CALLIE: *(Peeks in.)* Oh God! We have to check her. She could still be alive.

*JACK and CALLIE exit and close hallway door.*

*Offstage muffled sound of CALLIE and JACK speaking.*

*GERALD goes to the kitchen, grabs several large knives.*

*The hallway door opens and JACK enters.*

JACK: Holy Cripes!

*JACK exits, slams door.*

*Offstage muffled sound of CALLIE and JACK speaking urgently.*

*GERALD picks up a chair, positions it with its back to a wall, sits.*

*JACK and CALLIE enter.*

JACK: How is it going? Not so good? I can relate.

GERALD: Stay back.

JACK: No problem. *(Beat.)* You want to hear about Libby? Or maybe you already know?

GERALD: One of you did…exactly what was waiting behind that door…

JACK: From what I just saw…for the first time…looks like she was strangled.

There's an extension cord wrapped around her neck. *(Cries.)* Sorry. I don't even want to think about the look on Trisha's face…

GERALD: We didn't hear a thing. Why not?

JACK: Good question.

GERALD: *(Indicates message on the whiteboard.)* And to say she deserved to die, if that's what that means. Because she fooled Chuck? Or, maybe, guilt by association? She said I'm the key; maybe I tainted her. I'm a poison.

CALLIE: I never should've come back. Never should've left my car in the first place.

*Callie's statement triggers an idea for JACK.*

*JACK exits into mud room.*

Where are you going?!

JACK: If you need help, yell loud.

*Sound of door to garage opening.*

GERALD: Should move her.

CALLIE: What?

GERALD: Can't leave her like that, on the floor. The indignity. *(Exits down hallway.)*

*JACK enters carrying several long orange outdoor power cords, a garden hose, some rope. He drops the items to the floor, starts tying them end-to-end to form one long chain.*

JACK: Where's Mr. G.?

CALLIE: Moving Libby.

JACK: Huh?

CALLIE: What's all that for?

JACK: My life-line back, if I can't make it to the truck.

CALLIE: You can't leave!

JACK: Thought you'd be jumping for joy to see the back of me.

CALLIE: Bastard!

*JACK gathers several blankets, goes to kitchen, hunts down a roll of tin foil, several candles and matches.*

JACK: It didn't do Alena or Libby no good, me being here. If Libby's forecast was right, tomorrow, New Year's Eve, the snow stops. I'll boot it to the nearest phone, get help.

CALLIE: I'll be dead by then. *(Beat.)* You'll never make it; trust me. *(Beat.)* You're really going to scurry off, leave me at his mercy?

JACK: I'm not so sure it isn't poor Gerry I'm leaving high and dry.

CALLIE: Or you're the killer, and this is some sort of trick.

JACK: You got me. I'm gonna knock you off from the truck. Got my crossbow in there; hang out by the window every now and again, will you?

GERALD: *(Enters, surveys scene.)* Jacobus. *Vade in pace.*

JACK: I'm going, but no way I'm going in peace. But, thanks.

CALLIE: *(Blocks JACK's path.)* I'm begging you.

JACK: Don't make me move you. Because I will.

*JACK exits. GERALD and CALLIE size each other up.*

GERALD: The sword hangs by a hair.

CALLIE: Assuming you're the killer.

GERALD: Assuming you're the killer.

*Blackout.*

## Scene 4 – Acta Est Fabula

*The wind shrieks.*

*GERALD and CALLIE each hold knives, sit wrapped in blankets with as much distance between them as possible. GERALD sits on his desk chair which has wheels.*

*They fight sleep, drink coffee, shake their heads, slap their cheeks, stand up and shake out their limbs.*

*GERALD stands and CALLIE adopts a defensive posture.*

*GERALD exits into mud room.*

*Sound of door to outside opening briefly.*

*GERALD enters, shivering, looking more alert.*

GERALD: Your father and Hal Rutledge were brothers?

CALLIE: That's right.

GERALD: What was his name? Did I teach him too? Treat him poorly?

CALLIE: You're really sick. Why keep pretending? Jack has been gone for hours. I know it's you.

GERALD: No I'm not.

CALLIE: Did you go crazy, living like a hermit, sifting through the Romans' bloody exploits? You've murdered two people, maybe three—was Mrs. Sturgeon the first?

GERALD: I can't keep my eyes open much longer. I'd really like to know why. *(Nods off, startles awake.)* Hail, Caesar, those who are about to die salute you.

*Silence.*

*GERALD slumps in his chair, his breathing deepens.*

*CALLIE watches him closely.*

*GERALD's knife drops to the floor and CALLIE winces at the clatter, but GERALD continues to sleep.*

*CALLIE cautiously approaches GERALD, takes the knife.*

*CALLIE studies GERALD briefly.*

*CALLIE grabs her coat, exits to mud room.*

*Offstage, sounds of wind howling louder as the door to outside opens and then closes.*

*Silence.*

*A few moments pass.*

*Offstage louder wind as the door to outside opens and then closes.*

*CALLIE enters holding about twenty feet of orange, outdoor power cord—both ends cut with a knife.*

*She holds the knife in her mouth and approaches GERALD.*

*CALLIE prepares the cord with a slip knot, drops a loop around GERALD and the chair back, quickly tightens the loop around GERALD—pinning his arms to his sides and tying him to the chair.*

Huh? What…? What are you doing?

*CALLIE loops the cord around his torso several times, then binds his legs to the chair.*

*GERALD kicks and struggles.*

Ah, it's freezing! You got it from outside.

CALLIE: What do you think, Smart Guy? Jack won't be finding his way back.

GERALD: *(Thunderstruck.)* The way you just said that, "what do you think, Smart Guy?"…That was Hal Rutledge's patented phrase, dripping with sarcasm. He wasn't your uncle.

CALLIE: You finally figured it out. But, too late.

GERALD: You're Hal Rutledge's daughter.

CALLIE: I used to be.

GERALD: It wasn't your aunt who just died…Velma was your mother!

CALLIE: I came straight here from the lawyer's office.

GERALD: You were stopped on the road—because you were coming here!

CALLIE: It wasn't easy finding the place, with all the snow. But when I was a kid, my dad used to drive us past here all the time; we'd spit out the windows, once in a while jump out and trash your mailbox. That's what I spotted, your old mailbox, "G. Goldie" on it.

I was about to pull into your laneway when all hell broke loose, cars skidding everywhere, old Mrs. Sturgeon hitting the ditch. I thought my plans were scuttled, but the others just enhanced everything.

GERALD: Your "plans"?

CALLIE: Are you really so dense? Just think of me as the hand of Morta, poised to cut your pathetic life-thread.

GERALD: But...why? Because I failed your father?

CALLIE: You destroyed his life; he destroyed mine.

GERALD: I destroyed his life?

CALLIE: You ground my father into dust. Told him he was worthless. All he ever wanted was to be a cop.

GERALD: His anger and violence pre-dated me; he would've been a monster in uniform.

CALLIE: So you intentionally derailed his life? Just another student to punish for your failures? You have no idea what you've done. I have the stuff of greatness; I knew early on. But what chance did I have for it to flourish?

GERALD: History...your dad's weakness, so you made it your strength?

CALLIE: He got me started down that road...tested me every, single day, in honour of you. When I made a mistake, he beat the daylights out of me. And he kept asking questions until I made a mistake.

GERALD: I'm sorry...

CALLIE: No you're not!

GERALD: I never failed a student—

CALLIE: —Save it, I know the line, "the student fails

himself". Once, maybe. But he comes back to you again…

GERALD: OK, you hate me, blame me…but why Alena… Libby?

CALLIE: The prof provoked me.

GERALD: What?!

CALLIE: Just because my studies are progressing somewhat slowly, she utterly dismissed me. But that just put her at the head of the list. And Libby's psychic guesses were getting a little too close for comfort. I drugged her; a couple of sleeping pills ground up and stirred into her tea. She was easy. I hadn't figured out how to handle Jack; it was good of him to seal his own fate. I can't leave any witnesses. Besides, it has been such fun tormenting you, watching you squirm.

GERALD: You're quite the actress, breaking into tears at the drop of a hat, leaving after Alena…

CALLIE: I hid along the east wall, out of the wind, did jumping jacks to keep warm.

GERALD: You moved Mrs. Sturgeon's body.

CALLIE: Dumped her outside, hid the blanket for future use.

GERALD: And wrote the messages on the whiteboard…

CALLIE: Yes, but I never put those lines in your notebook, that flew off the shelf. That must've been the Fates. I took it as a signal to proceed, that I was to serve as their instrument.

GERALD: Beware…one day the hand-maiden of the Fates, the next—their prey.

CALLIE: Oh, and I'll be taking all of your book material…

"Fata" is going to make a fine Master's thesis, maybe even cop me my PhD.

GERALD: You're like I used to be, no care for happiness, or love; you live like a Roman, vainly hoping to survive as a marble bust. Tell me what does it profit Caesar that we know his name?

CALLIE: It's how he lived, such that we do know his name, that's the point. It must've eaten you alive, teaching every day about people who mattered, knowing you'd be completely forgotten.

GERALD: Your father…he died young.

CALLIE: I was twelve. He was drunker than usual that night. He choked on his own vomit. I helped him.

GERALD: You… helped him?

CALLIE: I helped him to choke to death.

GERALD: You killed your own father! At twelve?

CALLIE: Not my real father. The bitter, twisted demon you created. *(Beat.)* This is the first time I've set foot back in Huron County, since that night.

GERALD: You never saw your mother again? I'm sure her death stirred up plenty.

CALLIE: Hey, I've got an idea. Let's have one of your famous quizzes today, Goldfinger. The stakes are very high. One wrong answer: you fail; you die.

GERALD: You're going to kill me anyway.

CALLIE: The others I had to dispatch quickly; you, I can make suffer. How about a dead easy one to start: during the Civil Wars, Pompey said of Caesar's men, "I am fighting wild beasts!" Why? Come on! It was at Dyrrhachium. *(Beat.)* Stumped already? Caesar's men were living on a substitute for bread, made of grass. *(Beat.)* At Gades in the Temple of Hercules, Caesar was heard to sigh impatiently. Why? Answer me! Caesar was gazing upon the statue of Alexander the Great, and was vexed that at an age when Alexander had already conquered the whole world, he had done very little.

If refuse to answer, you fail!!! *(Prepares to stab.)*

*GERALD bursts out laughing.*

What's so funny?

GERALD: I just figured it out…

CALLIE: Figured what out?

GERALD: "Who the gods wish to destroy, they first make mad."

CALLIE: What are you babbling about?

GERALD: You don't exist.

CALLIE: Let me disabuse you of that notion.

GERALD: Well you might exist, but you're not here. And you might not be anything like, well…you.

CALLIE: I've pushed you right over the edge.

GERALD: Actually I suspect I lost it some time ago. To make me face some kind of reckoning. Even down to Mrs. Sturgeon, the generous, inspiring teacher I wished I could be. Dreams within dreams…Dionysus run riot.

CALLIE: Let me assure you, this is a real knife, and it is really going to hurt.

*Offstage sound of door to outside slamming.*

GERALD: Ja—!

*CALLIE quickly pushes GERALD's mouth into the crook of her elbow to gag him.*

CALLIE: Jack?!

JACK: Be right there.

*Sounds of JACK going into the garage.*

CALLIE: Acta est fabula. *(Stabs GERALD several times in the back.)*

*GERALD struggles, yells against the gag, then goes still and silent.*

*CALLIE wheels GERALD into the hallway, exits.*

*CALLIE enters holding cut power cord, blood all over her hands and the knife.*

*CALLIE begins to sob.*

*JACK enters, holding an axe.*

CALLIE: Thank God you're here. He finally made his move… Somehow I managed to get the better of him. He went out and cut some of your cord, so you couldn't make it back.

JACK: That was a dummy line. I figured he'd try something like that.

CALLIE: Maniac! Oh God…blood…all over…

JACK: Guess I won't be needing this axe.

*JACK turns his back to CALLIE.*

*CALLIE raises her knife, moves toward JACK.*

Laurie.

*CALLIE freezes.*

*JACK spins around, raises the axe.*

Laurie Rutledge.

CALLIE: You got into my car.

JACK: Found everything: your mom's will; the paperwork changing your name to Calpurnia Piso…Caesar's wife, right? Your mom's letter saying sorry for letting your dad beat you, blaming Mr. G. for making him so mean.

*(Raises axe up high.)* But I don't care what you went through growing up, after what you done here. So drop the knife! Drop it!!

CALLIE: Libby's dream…you with the axe. *(Drops the knife.)*

GERALD: *(Enters, covered in blood.)* Help!

JACK: Mr. G.! *(To CALLIE.)* Over there, kneel down, face to the wall! Don't move! *(Kicks away CALLIE's knife, rushes to GERALD, keeps an eye on CALLIE.)* Ah, man! Hang in there. *(Races to kitchen, grabs a bunch of tea towels, rushes back to GERALD, applies towels to wounds.)*

GERALD: Ahhhh…!!

JACK: Sorry.

GERALD: Watch her.

JACK: Don't you worry. Thought you were a goner.

GERALD: I probably still am. Damn it!

JACK: *(Wraps a blanket around GERALD.)* We got to somehow get you to a hospital.

GERALD: God, it's terrible knowing what you'd do with another year, and not having one.

JACK: Don't talk like that.

GERALD: If I did…want to hear my resolutions?

JACK: Oh yeah. New Year's. Auld Lang bloody Syne.

GERALD: Fall in love. Finish the damned book; get it published. Apologize to a lot of people. I guess I could start with you.

JACK: Don't worry about it.

GERALD: Please.

JACK: OK.

GERALD: You were a real pain in the ass—

JACK: —This is your idea of an apology?

GERALD: But you've got a fine mind. And farming is a noble profession. I'm sorry.

JACK: You didn't say anything about the fashion industry.

GERALD: Don't push it.

JACK: You're forgiven.

*With JACK distracted CALLIE retrieves her knife, sneaks around behind him.*

GERALD: The wind is going to stop now.

*The wind stops.*

*The snow stops flying past in the window.*

JACK: Holy…

*GERALD smiles, lies still.*

Ah, no.

*CALLIE raises her knife to strike. Suddenly CALLIE's eyes are drawn to the window; she is stunned and mesmerized.*

CALLIE: Fata!

JACK: *(Notices CALLIE, leaps back.)* Hey!? Put that down! Now!!

CALLIE: Caesar welcomed death.

JACK: What are you doing?

CALLIE: Dismissed his Spanish bodyguards. Didn't want to grow old, weak. Better to die in a glorious, bloody flash, that would long be remembered.

JACK: You don't got to do this.

CALLIE: Victory or death!

JACK: Then get on with it. I got somewhere to be by midnight, if it's OK by the Fates.

*CALLIE and JACK raise their weapons, roar like lions, rush together.*

*Blackout.*

*Acta Est Fabula.*